Jimmie Johnson

ABDO
Publishing Company

A Big Buddy Book
by **Sarah Tieck**

VISIT US AT
www.abdopublishing.com

Published by ABDO Publishing Company, 8000 West 78th Street, Edina, Minnesota 55439.

Printed in the United States.

Coordinating Series Editor: Rochelle Baltzer
Contributing Editors: Heidi M.D. Elston, BreAnn Rumsch, Marcia Zappa
Graphic Design: Maria Hosley
Cover Photograph: *AP Photo*: Ken Sklute
Interior Photographs/Illustrations: *AP Photo*: Gene Blythe (p. 21), Bob Brodbeck (p. 17), Chuck Burton (p. 10), Pat Carter (p. 17), Dima Gavrysh (p. 25), Carolyn Kaster (p. 15), Wilfredo Lee (p. 23), David Maung (p. 13), Carlos Osorio (p. 5), Frank Polich (p. 19), Terry Renna (p. 23), Bill Scott/File (p. 29), Keith Shimada (p. 18), Matt Slocum (p. 9), Tom Strattman (p. 13); *Getty Images*: Greg Foster/Sports Illustrated (p. 7), Kent Horner (p. 27), Fred Vulch/ Sports Illustrated (p. 29).

Library of Congress Cataloging-in-Publication Data

Tieck, Sarah, 1976-
  Jimmie Johnson : NASCAR champion / Sarah Tieck.
    p. cm. -- (Big buddy biographies)
  ISBN 978-1-60453-709-3
  1. Johnson, Jimmie, 1975---Juvenile literature. 2. Stock car drivers--United States--Biography--Juvenile literature. 3. Automobile racing drivers--United States--Biography--Juvenile literature. I. Title.
  GV1032.J54T54 2010
  796.72092--dc22   9505
  [B]
                        2009011848

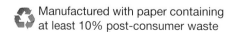

Contents

Racing Star

Jimmie Johnson is a famous race car driver. He races with the National Association for Stock Car Auto Racing (NASCAR). Over the years, Jimmie has won many races. He is considered one of NASCAR's top drivers.

Jimmie's driving skills have earned him many fans!

Family Life

Jimmie Kenneth Johnson was born in El Cajon, California, on September 17, 1975. His parents are Gary and Cathy Johnson. Jimmie has two younger brothers named Jarit and Jessie.

As Jimmie grew up, his father took him to local off-road races. Jimmie remains close with his family. They often attend his races.

Oregon

Nevada · Utah

PACIFIC OCEAN

California

Arizona

El Cajon

N
W · E
S

MEXICO

Jimmie grew up in a small house in El Cajon. This town is near San Diego and the Laguna Mountains. Jimmie's father was a truck driver and a construction worker. His mother drove a school bus.

Jimmie attended Granite Hills High School in El Cajon.

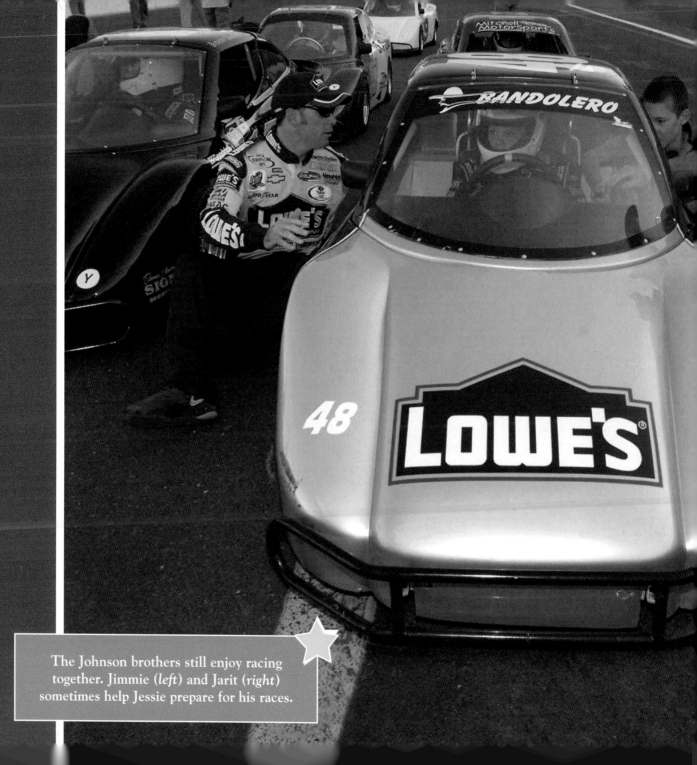

The Johnson brothers still enjoy racing together. Jimmie (*left*) and Jarit (*right*) sometimes help Jessie prepare for his races.

Early Years

Jimmie began racing when he was just five. His family often camped in the desert. There, the brothers raced dirt bikes and dune buggies in the sand.

To improve his racing skills, Jimmie practiced often. When he was eight, he won a local motorcycle racing championship. By age 12, Jimmie had started racing other vehicles.

Racing Dreams

As Jimmie got older, his interest and talent in racing grew. But in 1994, Jimmie's life changed during the Baja 1000 race. This race takes more than 20 hours to finish. After driving for many hours, Jimmie fell asleep and crashed his truck.

Jimmie had to wait almost two days for help. He thought about his racing **future**. He realized he needed to improve his skills to be successful.

Jimmie grew up racing off road on unstable surfaces. Many people believe this has helped him better control his car on paved racetracks.

Jimmie wanted to become a NASCAR driver. So around 1996, he moved to Charlotte, North Carolina. He hoped to have more racing opportunities there.

Jimmie got his start in the American Speed Association (ASA). The ASA holds **minor** racing **series**. Jimmie hoped to show he was ready for harder races.

Soon, Jimmie's talent was recognized. In 1998, Jimmie was named ASA **rookie** of the year!

In Charlotte, Jimmie made an effort to meet people who worked in racing. He knew this was important to becoming a NASCAR driver.

NASCAR

NASCAR is a **professional** stock car racing group. It was created in 1948 by Bill France Sr. He was a race car driver and a businessman.

NASCAR races take place on racetracks throughout the United States. Each driver is part of a team. Teams **compete** in different **series**. Drivers work their way up from **minor** to major series.

NASCAR has millions of fans! People travel across the country to watch these exciting races.

Dale Earnhardt Jr., Jimmie, Rick Hendrick, Jeff Gordon, and Mark Martin (*left to right*) work together. They are part of a successful NASCAR team.

Jimmie drives the number 48 Lowe's Chevrolet race car.

Fast Track

In 1999, Jimmie started racing in NASCAR's Busch **Series**. In 2000, he began **competing** full-time with the Herzog Motorsports Busch team.

Around the end of the year, Jimmie joined the Hendrick Motorsports team. In 2001, Jimmie raced in his first Winston Cup event. The Winston Cup is NASCAR's most important race series. In 2002, Jimmie raced full-time in this series.

Jimmie sweats a lot while racing. He loses five to six pounds (2 to 3 kg) per race from sweating!

Jimmie was not as **experienced** as other Winston Cup racers. Many people thought he was too young to be in NASCAR's biggest **series**.

But, Jimmie worked hard. He won many races and was often among the top ten drivers. Soon, Jimmie was considered a strong driver. But, he had yet to become a NASCAR **champion**.

Rising Star

In 2006, Jimmie won three major NASCAR races. Then toward the end of the racing season, his rank dropped to eight.

Jimmie worked hard to improve. He soon reached number one. Then, he won the Nextel Cup. This made him the NASCAR **champion**! From this point on, Jimmie worked to become even better.

Jimmie was the NASCAR champion in 2006 (*left*) and again in 2007 (*above*).

Where in the World?

West Virginia

Kentucky

Virginia

Tennessee

North Carolina

Mooresville

Charlotte

South Carolina

Georgia

ATLANTIC OCEAN

N W E S

Off the Racetrack

When Jimmie is not racing, he spends time with his family. In December 2004, Jimmie married Chandra Janway. They live in Mooresville, North Carolina. The rest of the Johnson family lives nearby. Jimmie and Chandra also have a home in New York City, New York.

Chandra was a model before she married Jimmie. Now she also spends her time helping others.

The Jimmie Johnson Foundation works with Habitat for Humanity. Sometimes, Chandra and Jimmie (*far right*) take part in projects.

Jimmie and Chandra like to help others. So in 2006, they started the Jimmie Johnson Foundation. It helps children and families in need throughout the United States.

Jimmie enjoyed winning the Sprint Cup.
He continues to improve his skills.

Buzz

Jimmie's racing success continued. In 2008, he won the Sprint Cup. For the third year in a row, Jimmie was the NASCAR **champion**! He is only the second driver to do this.

Jimmie Johnson is a rising star with a bright **future**. Fans expect great things from him!

Cale Yarborough is the first racer to be named NASCAR champion three times in a row. He won the Winston Cup in 1976, 1977, and 1978.

29

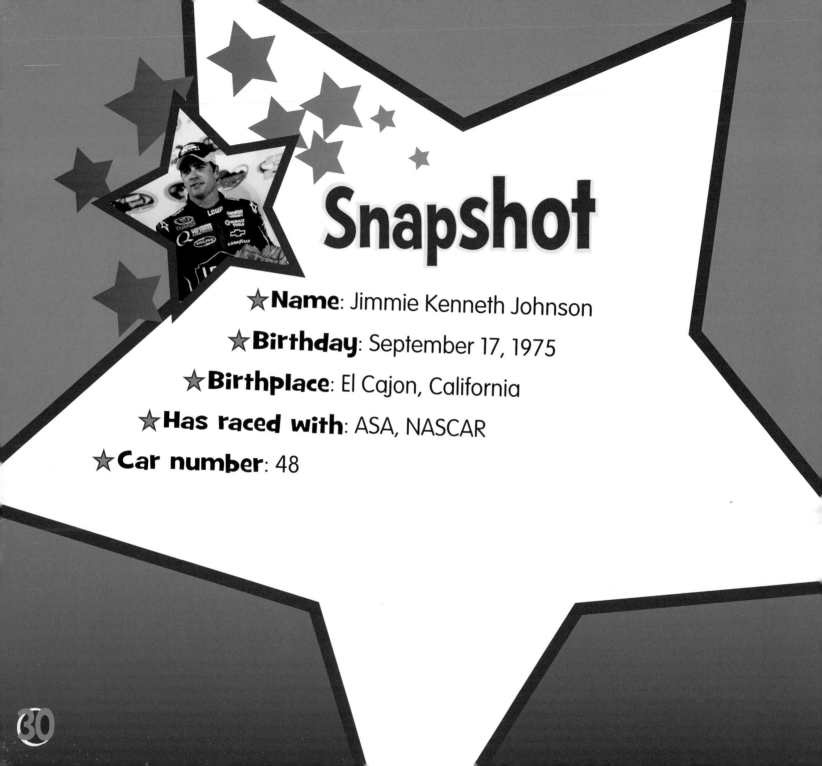

Snapshot

⭐ **Name**: Jimmie Kenneth Johnson

⭐ **Birthday**: September 17, 1975

⭐ **Birthplace**: El Cajon, California

⭐ **Has raced with**: ASA, NASCAR

⭐ **Car number**: 48

Important Words

championship a game, a match, or a race held to find a first-place winner. The winner is called a champion.

compete to take part in a contest between two or more persons or groups.

experienced having gained skill or knowledge through practice or work.

future (FYOO-chuhr) a time that has not yet occurred.

minor less in size, importance, or value.

professional (pruh-FEHSH-nuhl) working for money rather than for pleasure.

rookie a first-year player in a professional sport.

series a set of similar things or events in order.

Web Sites

To learn more about Jimmie Johnson, visit ABDO Publishing Company online. Web sites about Jimmie Johnson are featured on our Book Links page. These links are routinely monitored and updated to provide the most current information available.

www.abdopublishing.com

Index